main meals
IN 30 MINUTES OR LESS

Food and Styling DONNA HAY
Photography QUENTIN BACON

A J.B. Fairfax Press Publication

INTRODUCTION

This book is for all those people who want to feed themselves and their families well but need new ideas, inspiration and encouragement. It is all about solving the problem of creating great food in next to no time.

The recipes in this book make use of both fresh and convenience foods to create dishes that are interesting, yet not time-consuming to prepare. They range from the simplest open sandwiches (for when time is really short) to easy curries, main meal salads and fish dishes (all great for feeding a hungry family). Accompanying each main meal is a serving suggestion, so all the hard work really has been taken out of meal planning – all you have to do is cook and that will take you less than 30 minutes.

EDITORIAL
Food Editor: Rachel Blackmore
Editorial and Production Assistant: Sheridan Packer
Editorial Coordinator: Margaret Kelly
UK Food Consultant: Katie Swallow

Photography: Quentin Bacon
Food and Styling: Donna Hay
Home Economist: Jody Vassallo

DESIGN AND PRODUCTION
Managers: Sheridan Carter, Anna Maguire
Layout and Design: Lulu Dougherty
Cover and Chapter Design: Jenny Pace

Published by J.B. Fairfax Press Pty Limited
80-82 McLachlan Avenue
Rushcutters Bay, NSW 2011, Australia
A.C.N. 003 738 430

Formatted by J.B. Fairfax Press Pty Limited
Printed by Toppan Printing Co, Hong Kong
PRINTED IN HONG KONG

JBFP 304
Includes Index
ISBN 1 86343 143 8

DISTRIBUTION AND SALES
Australia: Newsagents Direct Distribution
Ph: (02) 353 9911 Fax: (02) 669 2305
Sales Enquiries: J.B. Fairfax Press Pty Limited
Ph: (02) 361 6366 Fax: (02) 360 6262
United Kingdom: J.B. Fairfax Press Limited
Ph: (0933) 40 2330 Fax: (0933) 40 2234

ABOUT THIS BOOK

INGREDIENTS
Unless otherwise stated the following ingredients are used in this book:

Cream	Double, suitable for whipping
Flour	White flour, plain or standard
Sugar	White sugar

WHAT'S IN A TABLESPOON?
AUSTRALIA
1 tablespoon = 20 mL or 4 teaspoons
NEW ZEALAND
1 tablespoon = 15 mL or 3 teaspoons
UNITED KINGDOM
1 tablespoon = 15 mL or 3 teaspoons
The recipes in this book were tested in Australia where a 20 mL tablespoon is standard. The tablespoon in the New Zealand and the United Kingdom sets of measuring spoons is 15 mL. For recipes using baking powder, gelatine, bicarbonate of soda, small quantities of flour and cornflour, simply add another teaspoon for each tablespoon specified.

CANNED FOODS
Can sizes vary between countries and manufacturers. You may find the quantities in this book are slightly different to what is available. Purchase and use the can size nearest to the suggested size in the recipe.

MICROWAVE IT
Where microwave instructions occur in this book, a microwave oven with a 650 watt output has been used. Wattage on domestic microwave ovens varies between 500 and 700 watts, so it may be necessary to vary cooking times slightly depending on the wattage of your oven.

CONTENTS

On the Run

PESTO PIZZETTAS

Oven temperature
200°C, 400°F, Gas 6

These pizzas are just as delicious cold as hot, so make extras and have them for lunch the next day.

4 small pitta bread rounds
$^1/_2$ cup/125 g/4 oz ready-made pesto
12 slices spicy salami
12 cherry tomatoes, halved
60 g/2 oz grated Parmesan cheese

1 Spread pitta bread rounds with pesto. Top with salami and tomatoes and sprinkle with Parmesan cheese.

2 Place bread rounds on a baking tray and bake for 10 minutes or until cheese melts and bread is crisp.

Serving suggestion: Serve with a salad of mixed salad greens, chopped black olives, chopped or sliced avocado and chopped or sliced tomatoes tossed with an Italian dressing.

Serves 4

TUNA TART

Oven temperature
200°C, 400°F, Gas 6

When rolling out pastry place it between sheets of plastic food wrap or baking paper. This saves on cleaning up and eliminates the problem of the pastry sticking to the work surface.

155 g/5 oz prepared puff pastry

TUNA TOPPING
2 spring onions, chopped
440 g/14 oz canned tuna in brine, drained
1 tablespoon chopped fresh dill
440 g/14 oz canned asparagus cuts, drained
2 tablespoons corn relish
$^1/_2$ cup/125 g/4 oz sour cream

1 To make topping, place spring onions, tuna, dill, asparagus, corn relish and sour cream in a bowl and mix to combine.

2 Roll pastry out to form a 25 cm/10 in square and place on a lightly greased baking tray. Spread with topping, leaving a 1 cm/$^1/_2$ in border around the edge and bake for 15-20 minutes or until pastry is puffed and golden.

Serving suggestion: Cut tart into squares and accompany with a salad of mixed lettuce leaves and chopped fresh herbs.

Serves 4

Previous page: Tuna Tart, Pesto Pizzettas
Opposite: Cheesy Noodles

CHEESY NOODLES

2 x 90 g/3 oz packets quick-cooking
noodles
4 tablespoons sour cream
freshly ground black pepper
60 g/2 oz tasty cheese (mature
Cheddar), grated

1   Prepare noodles according to packet directions. Drain, add sour cream and black pepper to taste and toss to combine.

2   Divide noodle mixture between two heatproof serving dishes and sprinkle with cheese. Place under a preheated hot grill and cook for 3-4 minutes until cheese melts and is golden.

Serving suggestion: Accompany with a salad made of the lettuce or lettuces of your choice, cherry tomatoes, chopped or sliced red or green peppers and chopped or sliced cucumber tossed with a French dressing.

Serves 2

Mixtures of fresh salad greens are available from many greengrocers and supermarkets. These are an economical and easy alternative to buying a variety of lettuces and making your own salads of mixed lettuce leaves.

Plate and bowl/Country Road Fork Alessi from G&C Ventura

HOT HAM SANDWICHES

2 x 10 cm/4 in squares focaccia bread
or 2 small French bread sticks
185 g/6 oz ricotta cheese, drained
250 g/8 oz smoked ham, sliced
60 g/2 oz sun-dried tomatoes, sliced
3 tablespoons chopped fresh basil
30 g/1 oz fresh Parmesan cheese
shavings

Split focaccia bread or French bread sticks horizontally and spread each half with ricotta cheese. Top with ham, sun-dried tomatoes, basil and Parmesan cheese shavings. Place under a preheated hot grill and cook for 3-4 minutes or until cheese melts and is golden.

Serving suggestion: Serve with a fresh mushroom salad. To make mushroom salad, place sliced button mushrooms and chopped red pepper in a bowl. Toss with lemon juice, olive oil, chopped fresh parsley or chives, minced garlic and a pinch of chilli powder. Set aside to marinate while preparing and cooking the sandwiches.

Serves 4

Cottage cheese can be used in place of ricotta cheese if you wish and fresh tomatoes or sliced black olives are good alternatives to the sun-dried tomatoes. To make Parmesan cheese shavings see hint on page 34.

GRILLED BANANA SANDWICHES

8 slices rye or Granary bread
2 bananas, sliced
1 avocado, sliced
8 slices Gruyère cheese

Place bread under a preheated hot grill and cook for 2-3 minutes or until toasted on one side. Top untoasted side with bananas, avocado and cheese. Place under grill and cook for 3-4 minutes longer or until cheese melts and is golden.

Serving suggestion: Serve with a cos lettuce and bacon salad. To make salad, grill 1-2 rashers bacon and break into pieces. Separate leaves of 1 cos lettuce, tear into large pieces and place in a salad bowl. Sprinkle with bacon pieces, 2-3 tablespoons croûtons and 2-3 tablespoons grated Parmesan cheese. Drizzle salad with a creamy dressing.

Serves 4

Tidying up as you go keeps you organised and will save time after the meal.

HOT CHICKEN SANDWICHES

Grilled Banana Sandwiches, Hot Chicken Sandwiches, Hot Ham Sandwiches

8 slices wholemeal or white
bread, toasted
4 tablespoons mayonnaise
500 g/1 lb cooked chicken, skin
removed and flesh shredded
440 g/14 oz canned asparagus spears,
drained
freshly ground black pepper
8 slices Swiss cheese, such as
Emmental or Gruyère

Spread toast with mayonnaise and top with chicken, asparagus, black pepper to taste and cheese. Place under a preheated hot grill and cook for 3-4 minutes or until cheese melts and is golden.

Serving suggestion: Accompany with a bowl of canned soup and a salad of mixed lettuces and chopped fresh herbs tossed with a French dressing.

Serves 4

Dress up canned soup by sprinkling with croûtons or fresh herbs. Prepared croûtons are available from supermarkets and are a useful ingredient to keep in your pantry for garnishing soups and salads.

Bowl and plate Country Road

SUN-DRIED TOMATO DIP

250 g/8 oz sun-dried tomatoes
60 g/2 oz pine nuts
3 tablespoons chopped fresh basil
3 tablespoons grated Parmesan cheese
250 g/8 oz cream cheese, softened
bagel chips or French bread, sliced
selection of raw vegetables such as
cherry tomatoes, celery sticks, carrot
sticks, broccoli florets, cauliflower
florets and green beans

Keeping a selection of bread in the freezer and bagel chips, corn chips and crackers in the cupboard ensures that you always have the necessary accompaniments for quick dips such as this one.

Place sun-dried tomatoes, pine nuts, basil, Parmesan cheese and cream cheese in a food processor or blender and process until smooth. Serve dip with bagel chips or bread and vegetables.

Serving suggestion: Place dip in a bowl on a serving platter or tray and surround with bagel chips or bread and/or raw vegetables.

Serves 4

10

SMOKED SALMON BAGELS

4 bagels, split
125 g/4 oz cream cheese, softened
2 tablespoons snipped fresh chives
250 g/8 oz smoked salmon slices
1 onion, thinly sliced
1 avocado, stoned, peeled and sliced
1 tablespoon capers, drained
1 tablespoon lemon juice

Spread each bagel half with cream cheese and sprinkle with chives. Top bagel halves with salmon, onion, avocado and capers. Sprinkle with lemon juice and serve immediately.

Serving suggestion: A tomato and onion salad is a delicious side dish. To make salad, arrange sliced tomatoes and very thinly sliced onion on a lettuce lined dish. Sprinkle with chopped fresh basil and drizzle with French dressing. Season to taste with black pepper.

Serves 4

Bagels are available in the bread or freezer sections of most supermarkets. Keep some in the freezer to have on hand for quick meals and snacks.

Left: Sun-dried Tomato Dip
Below: Smoked Salmon Bagels

Simply Seafood

SCALLOP AND PRAWN KEBABS

24 medium uncooked prawns, shelled
and deveined, tails left intact
24 scallops, cleaned

ORANGE AND SOY MARINADE
1 clove garlic, crushed
1 tablespoon honey
1 tablespoon soy sauce
1/4 cup/60 mL/2 fl oz orange juice
1 tablespoon vegetable oil
1 tablespoon chopped fresh mint

AVOCADO MANGO SALSA
1 mango, stoned, peeled and chopped
1 avocado, stoned, peeled and chopped
2 spring onions, chopped
2 fresh red chillies, finely chopped
1 tablespoon lemon juice
1 tablespoon chopped fresh coriander

1   Thread prawns and scallops,
alternately, onto lightly oiled skewers.

2   To make marinade, place garlic,
honey, soy sauce, orange juice, oil and
mint in a small bowl and mix to
combine. Brush skewers with marinade
and cook under a preheated hot grill,
turning frequently and brushing with
marinade until cooked.

3   To make salsa, combine mango,
avocado, spring onions, chillies, lemon
juice and coriander. Serve with kebabs.

Serving suggestion: Top naan or pitta
bread with lettuce, salsa and kebabs.
To eat, each person pushes seafood off
skewers, rolls up bread and eats in the
same way as you would a doner kebab.

Makes 8 skewers

If serving the kebabs as
suggested you may prefer
to remove the tails from the
prawns before cooking.
They will not look as
attractive, but will be easier
for people to manage.

GRILLED TUNA AND VEGETABLES

3 tablespoons olive oil
2 tablespoons balsamic or
red wine vinegar
1 tablespoon chopped fresh basil
freshly ground black pepper
4 baby eggplant (aubergines), halved
4 plum (egg or Italian) tomatoes,
halved
1 leek, cut into 7.5 cm/3 in pieces and
halved
4 tuna steaks

1   Place oil, vinegar, basil and black
pepper to taste in a bowl and whisk to
combine. Brush eggplant (aubergines),
tomatoes, leek and tuna with vinegar
mixture.

2   Heat a lightly oiled char-grill or
frying pan over a high heat, add
vegetables and tuna and cook,
brushing frequently with remaining
vinegar mixture, for 2 minutes each
side or until vegetables and tuna are
cooked. To serve, arrange vegetables
and tuna on serving plates and serve
immediately.

Serves 4

When cooking fresh tuna
take care not to overcook
it. The experts recommend
that you cook tuna so that
it is still pink inside. If tuna is
unavailable this recipe can
be made using swordfish or
salmon.

*Previous page: Scallop and Prawn Kebabs,
Grilled Tuna and Vegetables*
Plates Country Road and Pillivuyt from Hale Imports
Cane table Corso de Fiori

 text: *Plate Country Road Cane table Corso de Fiori*

Tomato Basil Trout

TOMATO BASIL TROUT

2 teaspoons vegetable oil
4 spring onions, chopped
1 clove garlic, crushed
4 small trout, cleaned
$^3/4$ cup/185 mL/6 fl oz red wine
4 tomatoes, chopped
4 tablespoons chopped fresh basil
freshly ground black pepper

Serves 4

Heat oil in a large frying pan, add spring onions and garlic and cook for 1 minute. Add trout to pan, pour over wine and top with tomatoes, basil and black pepper to taste. Cover and simmer for 10 minutes or until fish flakes when test with a fork.

Serving suggestion: Vegetables and crispy potato wedges are the perfect accompaniment to this dish. To make potato wedges, cut small potatoes into wedges and boil or microwave until tender. Drain and pat dry. Toss potatoes with $^1/4$ teaspoon chilli powder, 1 teaspoon ground turmeric, $^1/2$ teaspoon garam masala, 1 teaspoon ground coriander and $^1/2$ teaspoon ground ginger to coat. Shallow-fry for 5-10 minutes or until potatoes are crisp.

Trout freezes well and keeping a few trout in your freezer ensures that you always have a basis for a tasty meal.
Remember when freezing any fish or shellfish that it has a shorter freezer life than meat or chicken because of the higher proportion of polyunsaturated fats in it. Frozen fish is best used within 3 months of freezing and should be cooked directly from frozen, this ensures that it holds its shape and retains its flavour and texture.

PARMESAN-CRUSTED FISH

4 firm white fish fillets
1/2 cup/60 g/2 oz flour
1 teaspoon paprika
freshly ground pepper
1 cup/125 g/4 oz dried breadcrumbs
90 g/3 oz grated Parmesan cheese
1 egg, lightly beaten
2 tablespoons olive oil

LEMON THYME BUTTER
60 g/2 oz butter
1 tablespoon grated lemon rind
1 tablespoon lemon juice
1 tablespoon chopped fresh thyme or
lemon thyme

1   Pat fish dry. Combine flour, paprika and black pepper to taste. Combine breadcrumbs and Parmesan cheese. Coat fillets with flour mixture. Dip in egg, then coat with breadcrumb mixture. Heat oil in a frying pan over a medium heat, add fillets and cook for 2-3 minutes each side or until cooked.

2   To make Lemon Thyme Butter, heat butter, lemon rind, lemon juice and thyme in a saucepan over a medium heat for 1 minute or until butter melts. Serve with fish fillets.

Serving suggestion: Accompany with potato crisps and vegetables. To make crisps, using a vegetable peeler, peel thin slices from potatoes. Dry slices and deep-fry for 7-10 minutes or until cooked. Drain and sprinkle with salt.

When buying fish fillets, look for those that are shiny and firm with a pleasant sea smell. Avoid fillets that are dull, soft, discoloured or 'ooze' water when touched.

Serves 4

Plates Waterford Wedgwood

SALMON WITH MUSTARD SAUCE

Left: Parmesan-crusted Fish
Above: Salmon with Mustard Sauce

2 small cucumbers
2 cups/500 mL/16 fl oz water
^{1}/4 cup/60 mL/2 fl oz white wine
1 tablespoon finely grated lime rind
2 fresh dill sprigs
4 salmon cutlets

MUSTARD SAUCE
^{1}/2 cup/125 g/4 oz whole egg
mayonnaise
2 tablespoons wholegrain mustard
1 tablespoon lemon juice

1 Using a vegetable peeler, cut cucumber into long strips and set aside.

2 Place water, wine, lime rind and dill in a large deep frying pan and bring to the boil over a medium heat. Reduce heat to simmering, add salmon and cook for 5-6 minutes or until fish flakes when tested with a fork.

3 To make sauce, place mayonnaise, mustard and lemon juice in a bowl and mix to combine.

4 To serve, line serving plates with a bed of cucumber strips, top with salmon cutlets and sauce.

Serving suggestion: For a complete meal serve with crusty bread or wholemeal rolls and finish with a selection of seasonal fresh fruit or a cheese board.

Serves 4

Special enough for a birthday or anniversary, yet easy enough to cook when guests arrive unexpectedly. For a special occasion start with a tossed green salad and finish with Summer Fruits in Wine (page 64) or Peach Crumble Tart (page 66) depending on the season.

SPEEDY BOUILLABAISSE

2 teaspoons olive oil
2 onions, chopped
2 cloves garlic, crushed
1 fresh red chilli, chopped
250 g/8 oz uncooked medium prawns,
peeled and deveined
16 mussels, scrubbed and beards
removed
16 scallops, cleaned
440 g/14 oz canned spicy tomato soup
2 cups/500 mL/16 fl oz fish or
chicken stock
125 g/4 oz squid (calamari) rings
2 tablespoons chopped fresh mixed
herbs

For this recipe there is no
need to be too exact
about the type and
quantity of seafood that
you use. It is delicious made
with any fish or seafood so
use the recipe as a guide
only.

1 Heat oil in a large frying pan over a
medium heat, add onions, garlic and
chilli and cook, stirring, for 4 minutes
or until onions are soft.

2 Add prawns and cook for 1 minute.
Add mussels, scallops, soup and stock
and bring to simmering.

3 Stir in squid (calamari) and herbs
and cook for 1 minute longer or until
seafood is cooked.

Serving suggestion: Serve with quick-
cooking brown rice or pasta.

Serves 4

CHILLI TEMPURA

vegetable oil for deep-frying
500 g/1 lb uncooked large prawns,
peeled and deveined, tails left intact
12 snow peas (mangetout), trimmed
1 red pepper, cut into large squares
1 small head broccoli, broken into
small florets

TEMPURA BATTER
3/4 cup/90 g/3 oz self-raising flour
1/2 cup/60 g/2 oz cornflour
1 teaspoon chilli powder
1 egg, lightly beaten
1 cup/250 mL/8 fl oz iced water
4 ice cubes

Supermarkets have a wide
range of sauces, chutneys
and relishes that make tasty
accompaniments to this
dish. For more unusual ideas
pay a visit to a speciality
Oriental food shop.

1 To make batter, place flour,
cornflour and chilli powder in a bowl,
mix to combine and make a well in the
centre. Whisk in egg and water and
beat until smooth. Add ice cubes.

2 Heat oil in a deep saucepan until a
cube of bread dropped in browns in 50
seconds.

3 Dip prawns, snow peas (mangetout),
red pepper pieces and broccoli florets
in batter and deep-fry a few at a time
for 3-4 minutes or until golden and
crisp. Serve immediately.

Serving suggestion: All that is needed
to make this a complete meal is a
variety of purchased dipping sauces,
chutneys and relishes and a tossed

Serves 4 green salad.

Speedy Bouillabaisse, Chilli Tempura

Plate Country Road Cutlery Alessi from G&C Ventura

Above: Seafood Salad
Right: Cod in a Bag

SEAFOOD SALAD

375 g/12 oz calamari (squid) rings
1 tablespoon olive oil
375 g/12 oz uncooked medium
prawns, peeled and deveined
1 clove garlic, crushed
1 bunch/500 g/1 lb English spinach
1 red onion, sliced
1 red pepper, cut into strips
250 g/8 oz snow peas (mangetout),
trimmed
2 tablespoons fresh mint leaves
30 g/1 oz nuts, finely chopped

CHILLI DRESSING
2 tablespoons sweet chilli sauce
1 tablespoon soy sauce
1 tablespoon lime juice
1 tablespoon vegetable oil

When buying fresh calamari (squid) it should have a good colour, a slippery appearance and a fresh salty smell. Avoid calamari (squid) that have broken outer skins or those that are lying in a pool of ink.

Serves 4

1 Place calamari (squid) on absorbent kitchen paper and pat dry.

2 Heat oil in a frying pan over a medium heat, add prawns and garlic and stir-fry for 2 minutes. Add squid (calamari) and stir-fry for 2 minutes longer. Set aside to cool.

3 Arrange spinach leaves, onion, red pepper, snow peas (mangetout), mint and nuts in a bowl or on a serving platter. Top with seafood mixture.

4 To make dressing, place chilli sauce, soy sauce, lime juice and oil in a bowl and mix to combine. Spoon dressing over salad and chill.

Serving suggestion: This dish only requires fresh crusty bread or rolls. In summer finish with Caramel Chip Ice Cream (page 67).

COD IN A BAG

45 g/1¹/₂ oz butter
2 teaspoons ground cumin
2 teaspoons finely grated lime rind
1 tablespoon lime juice
1 fresh red chilli, finely chopped
2 tablespoons chopped fresh coriander
4 tablespoons pine nuts
4 cod cutlets

1   Melt butter in a frying pan, add cumin and cook for 1 minute. Add lime rind, lime juice, chilli, coriander and pine nuts and cook, stirring, for 1 minute.

2   Cut eight circles of nonstick baking paper large enough to enclose cutlets. For each cutlet, layer two pieces of paper, place a cutlet on one half and top with one-quarter of the lime mixture. Fold paper over and roll edges to seal. Cook parcels on a baking tray for 10-15 minutes.

Serving suggestion: Serve with sautéed potatoes and a snow pea (mangetout) salad. To make salad, cook snow peas (mangetout) until just tender. Refresh under cold water and drain. Combine 1 clove crushed garlic, 2 tablespoons lemon juice, ¹/₂ teaspoon dry mustard, 2 tablespoons dry sherry, 3 tablespoons vegetable oil and ¹/₄ teaspoon minced red chillies, pour over snow peas (mangetout) and toss to combine. Sprinkle with chopped spring onion and finely chopped red pepper.

Serves 4

Oven temperature
200°C, 400°F, Gas 6

Cooking fish in paper prevents it from drying out and nearly all types of fish are suitable to cook this way. The fish is cooked when the paper browns and puffs up. The best part of cooking fish this way is when you open the parcel and release the rich aroma that has formed during cooking. The French call this method of cooking *en papillote*.

Peppered Salmon

4 salmon cutlets
30 g/1 oz butter

BLACK PEPPER MARINADE
2 tablespoons coarsely cracked black
peppercorns
2 tablespoons chopped fresh dill
2 tablespoons lemon juice

LIME YOGURT
2 tablespoons snipped fresh chives
2 tablespoons lime juice
1 tablespoon finely grated lime rind
2 teaspoons honey
1 1/4 cups/250 g/8 oz low-fat
natural yogurt

Salmon is an oily fish which means that it has more Omega-3 fatty acids than white fish such as sole, plaice or whiting. Medical research has shown that Omega-3 has a lowering effect on blood pressure and blood fats.

1   To make Lime Yogurt, place chives, lime juice, lime rind, honey and yogurt in a bowl and mix well to combine. Cover and chill until required.

2   To make marinade, place black peppercorns, dill and lemon juice in a plastic food bag. Add salmon and shake to coat. Marinate for 5 minutes.

3   Melt butter in a frying pan over a medium heat, add salmon and cook for 2-3 minutes each side or until fish flakes when tested with a fork. Serve with Lime Yogurt.

Serving suggestion: This dish only needs the simplest of accompaniments. Bread and a salad of mixed lettuces tossed with balsamic or red wine vinegar is perfect.

Serves 4

Plate Country Road

Left: Peppered Salmon
Above: Lobster with Mint Pesto

Lobster with Mint Pesto

2 uncooked lobster tails, halved lengthwise

MINT PESTO
**1 bunch fresh mint
4 tablespoons almonds, toasted
1 clove garlic, crushed
$^1/4$ cup/60 mL/2 fl oz lime juice
$^1/4$ cup/60 mL/2 fl oz olive oil**

1 To make pesto, place mint leaves, almonds, garlic and lime juice in a food processor or blender and process to finely chop. With machine running, slowly add oil and process to make a smooth paste.

2 Place lobster on a baking tray, spread flesh with pesto and bake for 15-20 minutes or until lobster is cooked.

Serving suggestion: This dish is perfect for a special occasion meal. Start with an antipasto platter – purchase the ingredients from the delicatessen section of your supermarket. Accompany lobster with boiled new potatoes tossed with olive oil and black pepper and a salad of assorted lettuces and chopped fresh herbs. Finish the meal with a good quality purchased ice cream topped with a tablespoon of your favourite liqueur.

Serves 4

Oven temperature
200°C, 400°F, Gas 6

This dish is perfect for a special occasion such as a birthday or wedding anniversary. It is just as easy to make for two in which case you will only need one lobster tail. Any leftover pesto is delicious used on sandwiches or mixed with mayonnaise and used as a dressing for salads.

Salad Delights

SMOKED SALMON AND BRIE SALAD

1 bunch/250 g/8 oz watercress, broken into sprigs
315 g/10 oz assorted lettuce leaves
250 g/8 oz smoked salmon slices
1 avocado, stoned, peeled and sliced
250 g/8 oz Brie cheese, sliced
1 nashi pear, apple or pear, cored and sliced
250 g/8 oz asparagus spears, cut into 5 cm/2 in pieces, blanched
60 g/2 oz croûtons

MUSTARD AND HONEY DRESSING
1 tablespoon honey
2 tablespoons wine vinegar
1 tablespoon wholegrain mustard
$^1/4$ cup/60 mL/2 fl oz olive oil

1   Divide watercress and lettuce leaves between serving plates. Top with salmon, avocado, Brie cheese, nashi pear, apple or pear, asparagus and croûtons.

2   To make dressing, place honey, vinegar, mustard and oil in a bowl and whisk to combine. Spoon dressing over salad and serve immediately.

Serving suggestion: Accompany with warm herb bread. To make herb bread, place chopped fresh herbs and softened butter in a bowl and beat until smooth. Slice a French bread stick at 2 cm/$^3/4$ in intervals and spread one side of each slice with butter, wrap in foil and bake at 180°C/350°F/Gas 4 for 15 minutes.

Serves 4

> The secret to serving any of the salads of this chapter is in the presentation. It really takes no longer to arrange food attractively on a plate.

RAVIOLI AND PARMESAN SALAD

500 g/1 lb broccoli, broken into small florets, blanched
315 g/10 oz spinach ravioli, cooked and cooled
4 rashers bacon, grilled and broken into pieces
250 g/8 oz yellow teardrop or red cherry tomatoes, halved
125 g/4 oz sun-dried or roasted red pepper, sliced
3 tablespoons chopped fresh basil
3 tablespoons pine nuts, toasted

PARMESAN DRESSING
1 clove garlic, crushed
1 egg, lightly beaten
60 g/2 oz grated Parmesan cheese
1 tablespoon red wine vinegar
few drops Tabasco sauce
freshly ground black pepper
$^1/2$ cup/125 mL/4 fl oz olive oil

1   Boil, steam or microwave broccoli until it just changes colour. Drain and refresh under cold running water. Drain again and pat dry.

2   Place broccoli, ravioli, bacon, tomatoes, red pepper, basil and pine nuts in a bowl and toss to combine.

3   To make dressing, place garlic, egg, Parmesan cheese, vinegar, Tabasco sauce and black pepper to taste in a food processor or blender and process until smooth. With maching running, slowly add oil and process until creamy. Spoon dressing over salad, cover and chill.

Serving suggestion: Accompany with crusty bread rolls.

Serves 4

> The only time you should rinse cooked pasta under cold water is when you are using it in a salad. This prevents it from sticking together. When cooking pasta, always cook extra then you will have enough to make a salad for dinner the next night.

SMOKED CHICKEN SALAD

1.5 kg/3 lb smoked chicken, skin removed and flesh shredded
2 red peppers, roasted and cut into thin strips
2 yellow peppers, roasted and cut into thin strips
2 green peppers, roasted and cut into thin strips
250 g/8 oz cherry tomatoes, halved
1 cos lettuce, leaves separated and torn into pieces

BASIL DRESSING
3 tablespoons French dressing
$^{1}/_{2}$ cup/125 g/4 oz mayonnaise
1 tablespoon wholegrain mustard
2 tablespoons chopped fresh basil

1 Arrange chicken, red peppers, yellow peppers, green peppers, tomatoes and lettuce attractively in a salad bowl or on a serving platter.

2 To make dressing, place French dressing, mayonnaise, mustard and basil in a small bowl and mix to combine. Spoon dressing over salad and serve immediately.

Serving suggestion: Accompany with toasted rye or wholemeal bread.

Serves 4

Smoked chicken is one of the more recent food products and is available from some supermarkets and delicatessens. It has been cured and smoked and has a pale pink flesh with a delicate flavour.

Bowl and plate Pillivuyt

MEDITERRANEAN CHICKPEA SALAD

1 tablespoon olive oil
2 cloves garlic, crushed
2 x 440 g/14 oz canned chickpeas, drained
2 tablespoons chopped fresh rosemary
90 g/3 oz sun-dried tomatoes, sliced
125 g/4 oz marinated eggplant (aubergines), sliced
125 g/4 oz pitted marinated olives
250 g/8 oz feta cheese, crumbled
125 g/4 oz rocket or watercress
1 tablespoon olive oil
3 tablespoons balsamic or red wine vinegar

1 Heat oil in a frying pan over a medium heat, add garlic, chickpeas and rosemary and cook, stirring, for 5 minutes. Remove pan from heat and set aside to cool slightly.

2 Place chickpea mixture, sun-dried tomatoes, eggplant (aubergines), olives, feta cheese and rocket or watercress in a bowl and toss to combine. Sprinkle with olive oil and vinegar.

Serving suggestion: Serve with thick slices of fresh wholemeal bread.

Serves 4

Canned ratatouille can be used in place of the marinated eggplant (aubergines) if you wish.

Plate Country Road

CHICKEN AND PENNE SALAD

Left: Mediterranean Chickpea
Salad
Above: Chicken and Penne Salad

500 g/1 lb penne, cooked
1 kg/2 lb cooked chicken, skin
removed and flesh shredded
1 green pepper, chopped
3 tablespoons snipped fresh chives
440 g/14 oz canned sweet corn
kernels, drained
2 stalks celery, chopped
250 g/8 oz yellow teardrop or red
cherry tomatoes
250 g/8 oz curly endive
^{3}/4 cup/185 mL/6 fl oz creamy
salad dressing

Arrange penne, chicken, green pepper, chives, sweet corn, celery, tomatoes and endive on a large serving platter or in a large salad bowl. Spoon dressing over salad and serve immediately.

Serving suggestion: This salad is delicious served with chilli toast cheese. To make toast cheese, trim crusts from slices of white or wholemeal bread and cook under a preheated medium grill for 2-3 minutes or until toasted on one side. Top untoasted side with grated cheese and a pinch of chilli powder and cook for 2-3 minutes longer or until cheese melts and is golden.

Serves 4

29

THAI BEEF SALAD

2 teaspoons vegetable oil
1 clove garlic, crushed
1 tablespoon chopped fresh lemon
grass or 1 teaspoon finely grated
lemon rind
750 g/1¹/₂ lb rump steak, trimmed of
all visible fat, thinly sliced
2 tablespoons chopped fresh coriander
2 tablespoons lime juice
2 tablespoons sweet chilli sauce
250 g/8 oz bean sprouts
2 carrots, peeled and chopped
2 small cucumbers, thinly sliced
375 g/12 oz assorted lettuce leaves

1   Heat oil in a large frying pan over a
medium heat, add garlic, lemon grass or
lemon rind and steak and cook,
stirring, for 3 minutes or until steak is
tender.

2   Remove pan from heat, add
coriander, lime juice and chilli sauce
and toss to combine.

3   Arrange bean sprouts, carrots,
cucumbers and lettuce on a serving
platter, top with beef mixture and serve
immediately.

Serving suggestion: For a complete
meal accompany this popular salad
with warm naan bread. Naan bread can
be warmed in the microwave – 2 pieces
will take 30 seconds on HIGH (100%).

Serves 4

You will find naan bread in
the bread section of your
supermarket or it is
available from Indian food
shops.

CHEESE AND HERB SALAD

500 g/1 lb baked ricotta cheese,
chopped
2 tomatoes, cut into wedges
90 g/3 oz marinated olives
440 g/14 oz canned artichoke hearts,
drained and quartered
375 g/12 oz assorted lettuce leaves
4 tablespoons mixed fresh herb leaves,
such as coriander, parsley, sage
and chives
3 tablespoons balsamic or red wine
vinegar
185 g/6 oz croûtons

Arrange ricotta cheese, tomatoes,
olives, artichoke hearts, lettuce leaves
and herbs on a serving platter. Sprinkle
with vinegar, scatter with croûtons and
serve immediately.

Serving suggestion: Italian breadsticks
make an interesting accompaniment to
this Italian-inspired salad.

Serves 4

Baked ricotta cheese is
available from Italian food
stores and good cheese
shops. If it is unavailable
feta cheese is a good
alternative.

Thai Beef Salad, Cheese and Herb Salad

Winter Warmers

PASTA WITH ROCKET PESTO

500 g/1 lb fettuccine
fresh Parmesan cheese

ROCKET PESTO
250 g/8 oz rocket
60 g/2 oz pine nuts
30 g/1 oz grated **Parmesan cheese**
2 cloves garlic, crushed
3 tablespoons olive oil

1   Cook pasta in boiling water in a large saucepan following packet directions. Drain, set aside and keep warm.

2   To make pesto, place rocket, pine nuts, Parmesan cheese and garlic in a food processor or blender and process to finely chop. With machine running, slowly add oil and process until smooth.

3   Add pesto to hot pasta and toss to combine. Serve topped with shavings of Parmesan cheese.

Serving suggestion: To make a complete meal serve this tasty pasta dish with a sauté of eggplant (aubergines) and peppers. To make sauté, place a tablespoon of olive oil in a frying pan. Add 1 sliced onion and 1 tablespoon minced garlic and cook over a medium heat until onion is soft. Add 1 chopped eggplant (aubergine) and 2 sliced green peppers and cook, stirring frequently, for 5 minutes. Add 440 g/ 14 oz canned tomatoes and cook, stirring occasionally, for 10-15 minutes longer or until eggplant (aubergine) is soft.

Serves 4

To make Parmesan cheese shavings, you will need a piece of fresh Parmesan cheese. Use a vegetable peeler or a coarse grater to remove shavings from the cheese.

CREAMY TOMATO TORTELLINI

500 g/1 lb tortellini

CREAMY TOMATO SAUCE
2 teaspoons vegetable oil
1 clove garlic, crushed
4 spring onions, chopped
4 rashers bacon, chopped
440 g/14 oz canned tomatoes, chopped
1 tablespoon chopped fresh rosemary
or $^1/_2$ teaspoon dried rosemary
1 cup/250 mL/8 fl oz cream (single)

1   Cook pasta in boiling water in a large saucepan following packet directions. Drain, set aside and keep warm.

2   To make sauce, heat oil in a frying pan over a medium heat, add garlic, spring onions and bacon and cook, stirring, for 3 minutes or until bacon is cooked.

3   Stir in tomatoes, rosemary and cream, bring to simmering and simmer for 3 minutes or until heated through. Add hot pasta and toss to combine.

Serving suggestion: Serve with a salad of mixed lettuces and herbs or steamed vegetables of your choice and crusty bread rolls.

Serves 4

Bottled minced garlic, ginger and chillies are available from supermarkets. These save having to crush, chop and mince when time is short. If you have a good supply of garlic, chop a large quantity in the food processor when you have time to spare. To store, place chopped garlic in a screwtop jar, pour over enough olive oil to cover, seal and store in the refrigerator. The garlic will keep for about a month.

Previous page: Creamy Tomato Tortellini, Pasta with Rocket Pesto
Bowls Pillivuyt from Hale Imports
Opposite: Spicy Thai Soup

SPICY THAI SOUP

2 teaspoons vegetable oil
2 cloves garlic, crushed
2 tablespoons chopped fresh lemon grass or 1 teaspoon dried lemon grass or 1 teaspoon finely grated lemon rind
2 fresh red chillies, chopped
2 teaspoons finely grated fresh ginger
2 x 440 g/14 oz canned pumpkin or carrot soup
1 cup/250 mL/8 fl oz vegetable or chicken stock
1 cup/250 mL/8 fl oz water
1 cup/250 mL/8 fl oz coconut milk
2 tablespoons chopped fresh coriander
freshly ground black pepper

1 Heat oil in a large saucepan over a medium heat, add garlic, lemon grass or lemon rind, chillies and ginger and cook, stirring, for 2 minutes.

2 Stir in soup, stock, water and coconut milk and bring to the boil. Reduce heat and simmer for 5 minutes or until soup is hot. Stir in coriander and black pepper to taste and serve immediately.

Serving suggestion: Accompany this hearty soup with warm naan bread.

Serves 4-6

Keep a selection of bread in the freezer. It defrosts quickly and is a good accompaniment to any meal.

Plate Country Road Bowl/Pilliuvyt from Hale Imports Spoon Alessi from G&C Ventura

CHEESY PASTA BAKE

Oven temperature
200°C, 400°F, Gas 6

500 g/1 lb pasta of your choice,
cooked
220 g/7 oz tasty cheese (mature
Cheddar), grated
8 slices ham, shredded
250 g/8 oz button mushrooms, sliced
750 g/1¹/₂ lb jar tomato pasta sauce
2 tablespoons chopped fresh basil
30 g/1 oz breadcrumbs, made from
stale bread

For quicker preparation,
buy products that are partly
prepared – cubed meat,
grated cheese, instant
(no precooking required)
lasagne and boned
chicken. Many supermarkets
and greengrocers also sell
fresh salads and vegetable
mixes for soups and
casseroles.

1   Place hot pasta and 125 g/4 oz
cheese in a lightly greased ovenproof
dish, mix to combine and set aside.

2   Cook ham in a nonstick frying pan
for 3-4 minutes. Add mushrooms and
cook for 3 minutes longer. Spoon ham
mixture over pasta and top with pasta
sauce and basil. Combine breadcrumbs
and remaining cheese. Sprinkle cheese
mixture over pasta and bake for 20
minutes.

Serving suggestion: Accompany with a
broccoli and cauliflower salad. To
make salad, combine 2 tablespoons
lemon juice, 2 teaspoons Dijon
mustard, 3 tablespoons olive oil, 1
tablespoon finely chopped fresh parsley
and black pepper to taste and toss with
cooked broccoli and cauliflower florets.

Serves 4

Plate Pillivuyt from Hale Imports *Servers* Country Road

FAST LAMB CURRY

Left: Cheesy Pasta Bake
Above: Fast Lamb Curry

2 teaspoons vegetable oil
1 tablespoon curry paste
1 teaspoon ground cumin
500 g/1 lb lean lamb fillets, cut into strips
1 red pepper, cut into strips
2 zucchini (courgettes), sliced
250 g/8 oz broccoli florets
250 g/8 oz cauliflower, broken into small florets
1 cup/250 mL/8 fl oz coconut milk
$^1/_2$ cup/125 mL/4 fl oz beef stock

1 Heat oil in a wok or frying pan over a medium heat, add curry paste and cumin and cook, stirring, for 1 minute. Add lamb and stir-fry for 3 minutes or until lamb changes colour and is tender. Remove lamb mixture from pan and set aside.

2 Add red pepper, zucchini (courgettes), broccoli and cauliflower to pan and stir-fry for 2 minutes. Stir in coconut milk and stock, bring to simmering and simmer for 4 minutes. Return lamb to pan and cook for 2 minutes longer or until heated through.

Serving suggestion: Serve with rice or noodles and poppadums.

Serves 4

Cooked rice and pasta freeze well, they reheat in minutes in the microwave and save time on busy nights.

CHICKEN CHOWDER

Herb and garlic breads are easy accompaniments to soup and salad meals. Prepare ahead of time, wrap in foil and freeze. When needed, reheat from frozen. If you would prefer to serve herb bread see serving suggestion for Smoked Salmon and Brie Salad (page 26) for instructions on how to make.

30 g/1 oz butter
2 leeks, sliced
375 g/12 oz button mushrooms, halved
$^1/_3$ cup/45 g/1$^1/_2$ oz flour
$^1/_2$ teaspoon chilli powder
3 cups/750 mL/1$^1/_4$ pt chicken stock
1 cup/250 mL/8 fl oz water
2 cups/500 mL/16 fl oz milk
1 kg/2 lb cooked chicken, skin removed and flesh shredded
3 tablespoons snipped fresh chives
freshly ground black pepper

1   Melt butter in a saucepan over a medium heat, add leeks and cook, stirring, for 5 minutes or until leeks are soft and golden. Add mushrooms and cook for 2 minutes longer.

2   Stir in flour and chilli powder and cook for 2 minutes. Gradually stir in stock and continue stirring until mixture is smooth. Add water and milk, bring to simmering and simmer, stirring, for 5 minutes.

3   Add chicken, chives and black pepper to taste and cook for 3 minutes or until soup is heated through.

Serving suggestion: Accompany with warm garlic bread. To make garlic bread, see serving suggestion for Smoked Salmon and Brie Salad (page 26), but use crushed garlic in place of the herbs.

Serves 4

HEARTY POTATO AND BACON SOUP

2 teaspoons vegetable oil
1 large onion, chopped
6 rashers bacon, chopped
500 g/1 lb potato, peeled and chopped
2 tablespoons wholegrain mustard
185 g/6 oz canned sweet corn kernels
3 cups/750 mL/1$^1/_4$ pt chicken stock
1 cup/250 mL/8 fl oz cream (single)
2 tablespoons snipped fresh chives
freshly ground black pepper

1   Heat oil in a saucepan over a medium heat, add onion and bacon and cook for 4 minutes or until onion is golden and bacon crisp.

2   Add potato, mustard, sweet corn and stock and bring to the boil. Reduce heat and simmer for 10 minutes or until potato is soft. Stir in cream, chives and black pepper to taste and cook for 3 minutes or until heated through.

Serving suggestion: Pitta bread crisps are an easy accompaniment for soups. To make pitta crisps, split pitta bread horizontally, sprinkle with grated tasty cheese (mature Cheddar) and chopped fresh herbs and bake at 200°C/400°F/Gas 6 until bread is crisp. Break into pieces and serve with soup.

For a more substantial meal team soup with one of the sandwiches in On the Run (page 5).

Serves 4

Chicken Chowder, Hearty Potato and Bacon Soup

Above: Minestrone Soup
Right: Pasta with Tomatoes and Olives

MINESTRONE SOUP

2 teaspoons olive oil
1 onion, chopped
250 g/8 oz pasta shells
2 carrots, chopped
2 stalks celery, diced
1 red pepper, chopped
250 g/8 oz cauliflower, broken into small florets
440 g canned tomato purée (passata)
2 tablespoons chopped fresh basil
4 cups/1 litre/1³/₄ pt chicken stock
440 g/14 oz canned red kidney beans, drained
fresh Parmesan cheese

1   Heat oil in a saucepan over a medium heat, add onion and cook, stirring, for 2 minutes or until soft.

2   Add pasta, carrots, celery, red pepper, cauliflower, tomato purée (passata), basil and stock and bring to the boil. Reduce heat and simmer for 15 minutes or until pasta and vegetables are tender.

3   Add kidney beans and simmer for 5 minutes longer. Serve topped with Parmesan cheese shavings.

Serving suggestion: Accompany with herb or garlic bread. See serving suggestion for Chicken Chowder (page 38).

Serves 4

To make Parmesan cheese shavings see note on page 34.

PASTA WITH TOMATOES AND OLIVES

500 g/1 lb pasta of your choice
2 teaspoons vegetable oil
2 cloves garlic, crushed
8 slices spicy salami, chopped
4 tomatoes, chopped
60 g/2 oz pitted black olives
3 tablespoons chopped fresh basil

1   Cook pasta in boiling water in a large saucepan following packet directions. Drain, set aside and keep warm.

2   Heat oil in a frying pan, add garlic and salami and cook, stirring, for 3 minutes. Stir in tomatoes, olives and basil and cook for 3 minutes longer.

3   Place pasta in a serving bowl, spoon over sauce and toss to combine.

Serving suggestion: Accompany with a bean and artichoke salad. To make salad, combine cooked green beans with halved canned artichoke hearts and canned lima or butter beans. Combine 2 tablespoons olive oil, 4 tablespoons red wine vinegar and freshly ground black pepper to taste, pour over salad and toss to combine. Scatter with thin strips of red pepper.

Serves 4

A good pair of kitchen scissors is a must for the busy cook. They can be used to snip fresh herbs straight into dishes and are also good for cutting other foods such as chicken livers, dried fruit, bacon, ham and salami.

Plate Waterford Wedgwood

Family Favourites

GRILLED CHICKEN WITH PESTO

Chicken Parcels, Grilled Chicken with Pesto
Table Corso de Fiori *Cutlery* Alessi from G&C Ventura *Plates* Waterford Wedgwood *Napkin* Country Road

This recipe is ideal for cooking on the barbecue. Instead of cooking the chicken and vegetables in a char-grill or frying pan, simply cook on a lightly oiled preheated medium barbecue grill.

2 teaspoons vegetable oil
4 boneless chicken breast fillets
1 red pepper, quartered
1 green pepper, quartered
2 zucchini (courgettes), halved lengthwise
2 baby eggplant (aubergines), halved lengthwise

PESTO SAUCE
$^1/_2$ cup/125 g/4 oz ready-made pesto
$^1/_2$ cup/125 g/4 oz mayonnaise
2 tablespoons balsamic or red wine vinegar
freshly ground black pepper

Serves 4

1   Heat oil in a char-grill or frying pan over a high heat. Add chicken and cook for 4-5 minutes each side or until cooked through. Set aside and keep warm.

2   Add red pepper, green pepper, zucchini (courgettes) and eggplant (aubergines) to pan and cook for 2 minutes each side or until soft.

3   To make sauce, place pesto, mayonnaise, vinegar and black pepper to taste in bowl and mix to combine. To serve, arrange vegetables on serving plates, top with chicken and a spoonful of sauce.

Serving suggestion: Accompany with crusty bread.

CHICKEN PARCELS

Oven temperature
220°C, 425°F, Gas 7

Time saving starts with a well organised kitchen. Reorganising your kitchen, keeping the work surfaces free and having all your utensils to hand makes life easier.

15 g/$^1/_2$ oz butter
375 g/12 oz button mushrooms, halved
3 spring onions, chopped
1 kg/2 lb cooked chicken, skin removed and flesh chopped
$^3/_4$ cup/185 g/6 oz sour cream
freshly ground black pepper
500 g/1 lb prepared shortcrust pastry
1 egg, lightly beaten

1   Melt butter in a frying pan, add mushrooms and spring onions and cook for 3 minutes. Remove pan from heat, add chicken, sour cream and black pepper to taste and set aside.

2   Roll out pastry to 5 mm/$^1/_4$ in thick and cut out four 18 cm/7 in rounds.

Divide chicken mixture into four portions and place one portion on one half of each pastry round. Fold over other half of pastry and press edges to seal. Place parcels on a baking tray, brush with egg and bake for 15 minutes or until pastry is golden.

Serving suggestion: Delicious served with a salad of spinach and grilled bacon. To make salad, tear spinach leaves into pieces and place in a bowl. Scatter with grilled bacon pieces and chopped sun-dried tomatoes. Combine 2 tablespoons olive oil, 2 tablespoons balsamic or red wine vinegar and freshly ground black pepper to taste, spoon over salad and toss.

Serves 4

BURGERS WITH A LOT

Burgers with a Lot

500 g/1 lb lean beef mince
$^3/_4$ cup/45 g/1$^1/_2$ oz wholemeal
breadcrumbs, made from stale bread
1 egg, lightly beaten
1 tablespoon chopped fresh parsley
1 tablespoon vegetable oil
6 wholegrain rolls
4 tablespoons tomato relish
6 lettuce leaves
60 g/2 oz alfalfa sprouts
1 raw beetroot, peeled and grated
6 slices Swiss cheese such
as Emmental

1 Place mince, breadcrumbs, egg and parsley in a bowl and mix to combine. Shape mixture into six patties.

2 Heat oil in a frying pan over a medium heat, add patties and cook for 3 minutes each side or until cooked to your liking.

3 Cut rolls in half and toast under a preheated medium grill for 2-3 minutes each side or until golden. Spread bottom halves of rolls with tomato relish and top each with a pattie, a lettuce leaf, some alfalfa sprouts, some beetroot, a slice of cheese and top half of roll.

Serving suggestion: Accompany with oven fries and coleslaw. To make coleslaw, place finely shredded cabbage, grated carrot, chopped celery, chopped red pepper and grated tasty cheese (mature Cheddar) in a large bowl, add 3-4 tablespoons creamy or coleslaw dressing and toss to combine. Sprinkle with chopped fresh parsley.

Serves 6

Many fresh salads are available from supermarkets and delicatessans. When time is really short these salads are a great timesaver.

Above: Fish and Chips
Right: Super Steak Sandwiches

FISH AND CHIPS

500 g/1 lb oven fries
vegetable oil for shallow-frying
4 boneless firm white fish fillets

BEER BATTER
1 cup/125 g/4 oz flour
2 egg whites
³/4 cup/185 mL/6 fl oz beer
1 tablespoon vegetable oil

1 To make batter, place flour in a bowl and make a well in the centre. Add egg whites, beer and 1 tablespoon vegetable oil and mix until smooth.

2 Cook oven fries according to packet directions.

3 Heat 5 cm/2 in oil in a frying pan over a medium heat until a cube of bread dropped in browns in 50 seconds. Dip fish into batter, add to pan and cook for 3 minutes each side or until golden brown. Drain on absorbent kitchen paper. Serve with oven fries.

Serving suggestion: Accompany with a salad or vegetables of your choice.

Serves 4

Get to know your supermarket and write shopping lists according to the layout of the shelves.

SUPER STEAK SANDWICHES

2 teaspoons vegetable oil
2 onions, chopped
4 small lean rump steaks
4 canned pineapple rings, drained
8 thick slices wholemeal bread,
    toasted
4 slices tasty cheese (mature
    Cheddar)
8 slices tomato
4 lettuce leaves
tomato or barbecue sauce

Serves 4

1   Heat oil in a frying pan over a high heat, add onions and cook, stirring, for 2-3 minutes or until onions are soft. Push onions to side of pan, add steaks and pineapple rings and cook for 2 minutes each side or until steak is cooked to your liking.

2   Top 4 slices of toast each with a slice of cheese, 2 slices tomato, a lettuce leaf, a steak, some onions, a pineapple ring, a spoonful of tomato or barbecue sauce and remaining toast slices. Serve immediately.

Serving suggestion: Serve with oven fries or potatoes and coleslaw. To make coleslaw, see serving suggestion for Burgers with a Lot (page 45).

Steak sandwiches can also be cooked on the barbecue; rather than cooking in a frying pan cook on a lightly oiled preheated medium barbecue plate (griddle).

Plate Country Road Table Corso de Fiori

47

LAZY LASAGNE

Oven temperature
200°C, 400°F, Gas 6

1 x 90 g/3 oz packet white sauce mix
12 instant (no precooking required)
lasagne sheets
90 g/3 oz tasty cheese (mature
Cheddar), grated

SPICY MEAT SAUCE
2 teaspoons vegetable oil
1 onion, chopped
1 clove garlic, crushed
500 g/1 lb lean beef mince
500 mL/16 fl oz jar pasta sauce

When using instant (no precooking required) lasagne the cooked dish tends to be moister and the pasta more tender if the lasagne sheets are dipped in warm water before assembling the lasagne.

1 To make meat sauce, heat oil in a frying pan over a medium heat, add onion and garlic and cook for 2 minutes or until onion is soft. Add mince and cook, stirring, for 5 minutes longer or until meat is brown. Add pasta sauce, bring to simmering and simmer for 2 minutes. Set aside.

2 Make white sauce according to packet directions. Place 4 lasagne sheets in the base of a lightly greased ovenproof dish. Top with one-third of the meat sauce, then one-third of the white sauce and 4 lasagne sheets. Repeat layers finishing with a layer of white sauce.

3 Sprinkle with cheese and bake for 20-25 minutes or until hot and bubbling and top is golden.

Serving suggestion: Accompany with a green salad of mixed lettuces and chopped fresh herbs tossed with an Italian dressing.

Serves 4

MUSTARD-CRUSTED STEAKS

4 lean beef fillet steaks
2 teaspoons vegetable oil

MUSTARD CRUST
4 tablespoons wholegrain mustard
1 clove garlic, crushed
1 tablespoon honey
2 tablespoons mayonnaise

A food processor is the ultimate timesaver in the kitchen. Ingredients can be grated, shredded, chopped, blended, mixed and puréed in a fraction of the time it takes to do it by hand.

1 To make crust, place mustard, garlic, honey and mayonnaise in a small bowl and mix to combine. Spread mustard mixture over steaks.

2 Heat oil in a frying pan over a high heat, add steaks and cook for 2 minutes each side or until cooked to your liking.

Serving suggestion: An unusual accompaniment is broccoli with browned garlic. To make, divide a large head of broccoli into small florets, then boil, steam or microwave it until just tender. Refresh under cold running water. Divide a head of garlic into individual cloves and peel each clove. Heat 3 tablespoons olive oil in a frying pan, add garlic and cook, stirring, for 5-7 minutes or until garlic is brown. Take care that the garlic does not burn. Add broccoli to pan and cook, stirring, for 2-3 minutes or until heated. To complete the meal add mashed potatoes and finish with Caramel Chip Ice Cream (page 67).

Serves 4

Lazy Lasagne, Mustard-crusted Steaks

CHICKEN TACOS

12 taco shells, warmed
8 lettuce leaves, shredded
1 red pepper, thinly sliced
125 g/4 oz tasty cheese (mature Cheddar), grated
1 avocado, stoned, peeled and sliced
$^1/_2$ cup/125 g/4 oz sour cream

CHICKEN FILLING
2 teaspoons vegetable oil
1 onion, chopped
2 spring onions, chopped
3 tomatoes, chopped
1 kg/2 lb cooked chicken, skin removed and flesh shredded
2 tablespoons taco seasoning mix
4 tablespoons bottled tomato salsa

1   To make filling, heat oil in a frying pan, add onion, spring onions and tomatoes and cook, stirring, for 4 minutes. Add chicken, taco seasoning mix and salsa and cook, stirring, for 2 minutes longer or until heated through.

2   Spoon filling into taco shells and top with lettuce, red pepper, cheese, avocado and sour cream.

Serving suggestion: Accompany with a celery salad and crusty bread. To make salad, combine 2 tablespoons olive oil, 2 tablespoons white wine vinegar, 1 teaspoon Dijon mustard and freshly ground black pepper to taste, spoon over sliced celery and toss to combine.

Serves 4

Remember to make turning the oven on the first step when you are preparing a meal that requires you to cook in it.

PIZZAS

3 large purchased pizza bases
1 1/2 cups/375 mL/12 fl oz pasta sauce
or tomato paste (purée)
375 g/12 oz mozzarella cheese or tasty
cheese (mature Cheddar), grated

SUPREME TOPPING
8 slices ham, chopped
6 slices spicy salami
1/2 green pepper, chopped
125 g/4 oz canned pineapple pieces,
drained
125 g/4 oz button mushrooms, sliced
60 g/2 oz pitted olives (optional)

HAWAIIAN TOPPING
10 slices ham, shredded
185 g/6 oz canned pineapple pieces,
drained
1/2 red pepper, chopped

VEGETARIAN TOPPING
250 g/8 oz button mushrooms, sliced
1/2 red pepper, chopped
155 g/5 oz broccoli, broken into small
florets
1 small onion, sliced

1 To assemble pizzas, spread bases with pasta sauce or tomato paste (purée).

2 For Supreme pizza, top a prepared pizza base with ham, salami, green pepper, pineapple pieces, mushrooms and olives, if using.

3 For Hawaiian pizza, top a prepared pizza base with ham, pineapple pieces and red pepper.

4 For Vegetarian pizza, top a prepared pizza base with mushrooms, red pepper, broccoli and onion.

5 Sprinkle pizzas with cheese, place on baking trays and bake for 20 minutes or until base is crisp and golden.

Serving suggestions: All that pizzas require to make a complete meal is a tossed green salad.

Serves 4-6

Oven temperature
200°C, 400°F, Gas 6

Leftover pizza is delicious in packed lunches or can be frozen.

Plate Country Road

Left: Chicken Tacos
Right: Pizzas

ORIENTAL CHICKEN

4 boneless chicken breast fillets,
cut into strips
$^1/_4$ cup/30 g/1 oz cornflour
2 teaspoons sesame oil
2 teaspoons vegetable oil
1 clove garlic, crushed
4 spring onions, sliced diagonally
1 red pepper, chopped
375 g/12 oz canned baby sweet corn,
drained
250 g/8 oz broccoli florets
1 tablespoon oyster sauce
1 tablespoon barbecue sauce
2 tablespoons soy sauce

Serves 4

When buying chicken for a recipe which calls for boned chicken, buy breast or thigh fillets. These are more expensive, however, they are already boned and trimmed which saves you valuable time.

1 Place chicken and cornflour in a plastic food bag, toss to coat and shake off excess cornflour. Heat sesame and vegetable oils together in a wok or frying pan over a medium heat, add chicken and garlic and stir-fry for 3 minutes or until chicken is golden.

2 Stir in spring onions, red pepper, sweet corn, broccoli, oyster sauce, barbecue sauce and soy sauce and cook for 3 minutes or until vegetables are just tender.

Serving suggestion: Serve on a bed of quick-cooking noodles, quick-cooking brown rice or white rice.

RED WINE STEAKS

4 veal or pork steaks
2 teaspoons vegetable oil

RED WINE MARINADE
2 cloves garlic, crushed
$^3/_4$ cup/185 mL/6 fl oz red wine
3 tablespoons brown sugar
freshly ground black pepper

Serves 4

1 To make marinade, place garlic, red wine, sugar and black pepper to taste in a shallow glass or ceramic dish. Add steaks, turn to coat and marinate for 5 minutes. Turn over and marinate for 5 minutes longer. Drain steaks and reserve marinade.

2 Heat oil in a frying pan over a high heat, add steaks and cook for 1-2 minutes each side or until cooked to your liking. Remove steaks from pan, set aside and keep warm. Add reserved marinade to pan and boil until reduced by half. Spoon sauce over steaks and serve immediately.

Serving suggestion: Serve with peppered fettuccine and vegetables. For fettuccine, toss hot fettuccine with 1 tablespoon olive oil and 1 tablespoon coarsely crushed black peppercorns.

Oriental Chicken, Red Wine Steaks

No Meat Meals

BROCCOLI AND CHEDDAR SOUP

Previous page: Tostadas, Broccoli and Cheddar Soup

750 g/1^1/2 lb broccoli, broken
into florets
30 g/1 oz butter
1 clove garlic, crushed
1 onion, chopped
3 cups/750 mL/1^1/4 pt vegetable stock
^{3}/4 cup/185 mL/6 fl oz cream (double)
125 g/4 oz vintage or extra mature
Cheddar cheese, grated
1 tablespoon Dijon mustard

1   Steam or microwave broccoli until tender. Drain, refresh under cold running water and chop finely.

2   Melt butter in a saucepan over a medium heat, add garlic and onion and cook, stirring, for 3 minutes or until onion is soft. Stir in stock and cream, bring to simmering and simmer for 4 minutes or until heated through.

3   Add broccoli, cheese and mustard and cook for 1 minute longer.

Serving suggestion: Serve with bread rolls and finish the meal with a selection of fresh seasonal fruits or Peach Crumble Tart (page 66).

Serves 4

TOSTADAS

Oven temperature
200°C, 400°F, Gas 6

4 pitta bread rounds or tortillas

BEAN AND VEGETABLE FILLING
2 teaspoons vegetable oil
1 clove garlic, crushed
1 onion, chopped
3 spring onions, chopped
1 tablespoon ground cumin
2 x 440 g/14 oz canned red kidney
beans, drained
1 red pepper, chopped
1 cup/250 mL/8 fl oz ready-made
taco sauce
1 avocado, stoned, peeled and chopped
250 g/8 oz cherry tomatoes, halved
4 tablespoons sour cream
2 tablespoons chopped fresh parsley

When shopping look for new and interesting convenience products such as sauces and dressing, prepared pastries and pastry cases, canned fruits and vegetables and dessert items.

1   Place pitta bread rounds or tortillas on a baking tray and bake for 10 minutes or until crisp.

2   To make filling, heat oil in a frying pan over a medium heat, add garlic, onion, spring onions and cumin and cook, stirring, for 3 minutes.

3   Add beans, red pepper and taco sauce and cook for 4 minutes longer.

4   Divide filling between pitta bread rounds or tortillas, top with avocado, tomatoes, sour cream and parsley and serve immediately.

Serving suggestion: Serve with lettuce wedges. Cut a chilled iceberg lettuce into wedges and place in individual bowls. Combine ^{1}/2 cup/125 mL/4 fl oz lemon juice, ^{1}/4 cup/60 mL/2 fl oz olive oil and freshly ground black pepper to taste, spoon over lettuce wedges and serve immediately.

Serves 4

VEGETABLE CHEESECAKE

375 g/12 oz frozen spinach, thawed
250 g/8 oz cream cheese, softened
125 g/4 oz feta cheese, crumbled
4 eggs, lightly beaten
2 zucchini (courgettes), grated
1 carrot, grated
1 red pepper, chopped
freshly ground black pepper
60 g/2 oz tasty cheese (mature
Cheddar), grated

1   Place spinach in a sieve and squeeze to remove as much liquid as possible.

2   Place cream cheese, feta cheese, eggs, zucchini (courgettes), carrot, red pepper, spinach and black pepper to taste in a bowl and mix to combine.

3   Pour egg mixture into a greased 23 cm/9 in square cake tin, sprinkle with tasty cheese (mature Cheddar) and bake for 25 minutes or until set.

Serving suggestion: Serve with wholegrain rolls and a salad of mixed lettuces and chopped fresh herbs.

Oven temperature
180°C, 350°F, Gas 4

Also delicious cold this cheesecake is a tasty addition to any picnic and leftovers are always welcome in packed lunches.

Vegetable Cheesecake

Serves 4

Plate Swid Powell from G&C Ventura

VEGETABLE KEBABS

24 button mushrooms
4 zucchini (courgettes), cut into
3 cm/1¹/4 in slices
250 g/8 oz cherry tomatoes
6 spring onions, cut into
3 cm/1¹/4 in pieces
1 yellow or red pepper, cut into
3 cm/1¹/4 in cubes
16 baby bocconcini or 250 g/8 oz
mozzarella cheese, cut into
3 cm/1¹/4 in cubes

THYME MARINADE
2 teaspoons honey
1 tablespoon lemon juice
1 tablespoon chopped fresh thyme or
¹/2 teaspoon dried thyme
2 tablespoon olive oil

1   Thread mushrooms, zucchini (courgettes), tomatoes, spring onions, yellow or red pepper and bocconcini or mozzarella cheese, alternately, onto lightly oiled skewers.

2   To make marinade, place honey, lemon juice, thyme and oil in a small bowl and mix to combine. Brush kebabs with marinade and cook under a preheated hot grill or on a barbecue for 10 minutes or until vegetables are tender.

Serving suggestion: Serve with naan, pitta or Lebanese bread and a selection of chutneys and relishes.

Serves 4

When measuring honey rinse the spoon under hot water first, the honey will then slide easily from the spoon.

SATAY STIR-FRY

2 teaspoons vegetable oil
2 onions, cut into wedges
2 carrots, sliced
250 g/8 oz green beans, halved
250 g/8 oz broccoli, broken
into florets
250 g/8 oz cauliflower, broken
into florets
1 red pepper, chopped
3 stalks celery, chopped
60 g/2 oz unsalted cashews
1 cup/250 mL/8 fl oz ready-made
satay sauce

1   Heat oil in a wok or frying pan over a medium heat, add onions and stir-fry for 3 minutes or until onions are soft.

2   Add carrots, beans, broccoli, cauliflower, red pepper and celery and stir-fry for 5 minutes or until vegetables are just tender.

3   Stir in cashews and satay sauce and cook for 1 minute longer or until heated through.

Serving suggestion: Serve on a bed of quick-cooking noodles or quick-cooking brown rice.

Serves 4

The processing of quick-cooking brown rice involves soaking the rice, then draining and boiling or steaming it to gelatinise the starch. The rice is then cooled and dried. The end product is a light yellow-coloured rice that cooks in about the same time as white rice. This product is a must for any busy cook.

Satay Stir-fry, Vegetable Kebabs

ASPARAGUS AND CORN FRITTATA

6 eggs, lightly beaten
90 g/3 oz tasty cheese (mature
Cheddar), grated
315 g/10 oz canned sweet corn
kernels, drained
freshly ground black pepper
250 g/8 oz asparagus spears, trimmed
2 tablespoons chopped fresh basil
30 g/1 oz pecans, chopped

Place eggs, cheese, sweet corn and black pepper to taste in a bowl and mix to combine. Pour egg mixture into a lightly greased 23 cm/9 in round ovenproof dish. Top with asparagus, basil and pecans and bake for 20 minutes or until set.

Serving suggestion: Serve with thick slices of toasted rye or wholegrain bread and a salad of red lettuce and capers. To make salad, tear the leaves of a red lettuce of your choice into large pieces and place in a salad bowl. Combine 2 tablespoons balsamic or red wine vinegar, 1 tablespoon olive oil, $1/2$ teaspoon Dijon mustard and freshly ground black pepper, pour over lettuce, toss to combine and scatter with capers and croûtons.

A large pastry brush or small paint brush kept specially for cooking is useful for brushing foods with oils and marinades. Avoid brushes with nylon bristles as they can melt when they come into contact with hot food.

Serves 4

CHEESE AND SPINACH PIE

Left: Asparagus and Corn Frittata
Above: Cheese and Spinach Pie

2 x 375 g/12 oz packets frozen spinach, thawed
125 g/4 oz cream cheese, softened
250 g/8 oz feta cheese, chopped
60 g/2 oz tasty cheese (mature Cheddar), grated
$^1/_2$ teaspoon grated nutmeg
freshly ground black pepper
250 g/8 oz prepared puff pastry
1 egg, lightly beaten

1   Place spinach in a sieve and press out excess liquid. Place spinach, cream cheese, feta cheese, tasty cheese (mature Cheddar), nutmeg and black pepper to taste in a bowl and mix to combine.

2   Divide pastry into two equal portions and roll each out to form a 25 cm/10 in square. Place one pastry square on a lightly greased baking tray, top with filling leaving a 2.5 cm/1 in border around the edge. Brush edges with egg and place the other pastry square over filling. Press or crimp edges to seal and brush top of pie with egg. Bake for 20 minutes or until pastry is puffed and golden.

Serving suggestion: Delicious with herb toasts and a green salad. To make herb toasts, place softened butter, fresh dill, fresh parsley and freshly ground black pepper to taste in a food processor and process to combine. Spread butter over slices of French bread and bake at 200°C/400°F/Gas 6 for 10-15 minutes or until bread is crisp and golden.

Serves 4

Oven temperature
180°C, 350°F, Gas 4

A selection of cheese and fresh fruit served with wine is an easy entertaining idea for an impromptu get-together with family or friends. Don't forget to keep a selection of crackers to accompany the cheese.

Short and Sweet

BERRIES WITH BURNT CREAM

375 g/12 oz mixed fresh berries
2 tablespoons sugar
3 tablespoons orange flavoured liqueur
1 cup/250 mL/8 fl oz thick cream (double)
4 tablespoons brown sugar

1 Place berries, sugar and liqueur in a bowl and toss to combine. Divide berry mixture between four individual dishes.

2 Top fruit with cream, sprinkle with brown sugar and cook under a preheated hot grill for 3-4 minutes or top is golden.

Serves 4

This dessert should be served immediately it is ready and is delicious accompanied by dessert biscuits.

SUMMER FRUITS IN WINE

selection of summer fruits such as berries, nectarines, apricots, plums and peaches
$^1/_2$ cup/125 mL/4 fl oz sauterne or sweet white wine
1 tablespoon sugar

SAUTERNE CREAM
1 cup/250 mL/8 fl oz cream (double)
$^1/_3$ cup/90 mL/3 fl oz sauterne or sweet white wine
1 teaspoon vanilla essence

1 Peel, stone and slice fruit as necessary. Place fruit, wine and sugar in a bowl, toss to combine and set aside to macerate for 10 minutes.

2 To make Sauterne Cream, place cream in a bowl and whip until soft peaks form. Fold in wine and vanilla essence.

3 To serve, arrange fruit on serving plates and top with a spoonful of Sauterne Cream.

Serves 4

While this recipe specifies summer fruits it is delicious made with any fresh seasonal fruit. In winter you could use a combination of kiwifruit, bananas and apples.

Previous page: Summer Fruits in Wine, Berries with Burnt Cream
Plate Waterford Wedgwood
Opposite: Waffles with Caramel Apples

WAFFLES WITH CARAMEL APPLES

125 g/4 oz butter
³/4 cup/125 g/4 oz brown sugar
2 apples, cored, peeled and sliced
¹/2 cup/125 mL/4 fl oz cream (double)
8 waffles, toasted
4 scoops vanilla ice cream (optional)

1   Melt butter in a frying pan over a medium heat, add sugar and cook, stirring, for 2-3 minutes or until sugar melts and mixture combines.

2   Add apples and cook for 2 minutes. Stir in cream, bring to simmering and simmer for 4 minutes.

3   To serve, place 2 waffles on each serving plate, spoon over apple mixture and accompany with ice cream if desired.

Serves 4

For something different make this dessert using bananas or pears rather than apples.

Plate Country Road

65

Tiramisu

250 g/8 oz mascarpone
$^1/_2$ cup/125 mL/8 fl oz cream (double)
2 tablespoons brandy
$^1/_4$ cup/60 g/2 oz sugar
2 tablespoons instant coffee powder
1$^1/_2$ cups/375 mL/12 fl oz boiling water
1 x 250 g/8 oz packet sponge fingers
250 g/8 oz grated chocolate

1 Place mascarpone, cream, brandy and sugar in a bowl, mix to combine and set aside. Dissolve coffee powder in boiling water and set aside.

2 Line the base of a 20 cm/8 in square dish with one-third of the sponge fingers. Sprinkle one-third of the coffee mixture over sponge fingers, then top with one-third of the mascarpone mixture. Repeat layers finishing with a layer of mascarpone mixture, sprinkle with grated chocolate and chill for 15 minutes before serving.

Serves 4

Mascarpone is a fresh cheese made from cream. It is available from delicatessens and some supermarkets. If unavailable, mix one part sour cream with three parts lightly whipped cream (double) and use in its place.

Peach Crumble Tart

4 fresh or canned peaches, sliced
1 x 20 cm/8 in prepared sweet pastry case
4 tablespoons brown sugar

CRUMBLE TOPPING
1 cup/125 g/4 oz flour
90 g/3 oz butter
45 g/1$^1/_2$ oz desiccated coconut
$^1/_3$ cup/90 g/3 oz sugar

1 Arrange peach slices attractively in pastry case and sprinkle with brown sugar.

2 To make topping, place flour, butter, coconut and sugar in a food processor and process until mixture resembles fine breadcrumbs.

3 Sprinkle topping over peaches and bake for 20 minutes or until topping is golden and crisp.

Serves 4-6

Oven temperature
200°C, 400°F, Gas 6

Other fruits such as apricots, apples and plums can also be used to make this crumble.

Tiramisu, Caramel Chip Ice Cream

CARAMEL CHIP ICE CREAM

**2 litres/3¹/₂ pt vanilla ice cream,
softened
155 g/5 oz soft caramels, chopped
125 g/4 oz chocolate, chopped
chocolate or caramel topping (sauce)**

1   Place ice cream, caramels and
chocolate in a bowl and mix to
combine. Cover and freeze until firm.

2   To serve, place scoops of ice cream
in bowls and top with chocolate or
caramel topping (sauce). Serve
immediately.

Serves 6

Serve ice cream with
dessert biscuits of your
choice.

Something Special

SPRING DELIGHT

> MENU
>
> *Smoked Salmon and Brie*
>
>
>
> *Honey Rosemary Lamb*
> *Asparagus tied with Leeks*
> *Tomato and Thyme Salad*
>
>
>
> *Selection of Ice Creams and Fresh Fruits*
> *Truffles or Florentines*
> *Coffee*

There is no trick to mid-week and impromptu entertaining – it's simply a matter of careful planning. Here you will find two menus (complete with shopping lists and menu planners) that give the impression of having taken much longer to prepare then they actually do.

SHOPPING LIST

Take this list with you when you go shopping and you won't have to worry about forgetting an important ingredient.

- ☐ **4 racks lamb, each containing 3 cutlets**
- ☐ **125 g/4 oz smoked salmon slices**
- ☐ **125 g/4 oz Brie cheese**
- ☐ **rye bread**
- ☐ **selection ice cream**
- ☐ **truffles or florentines**

FRUIT AND VEGETABLES

- ☐ **1 avocado**
- ☐ **1 lime**
- ☐ **500 g/1 lb asparagus spears**
- ☐ **1 thin leek**
- ☐ **125 g/4 oz cherry tomatoes**
- ☐ **2 plum (egg or Italian) tomatoes**
- ☐ **125 g/4 oz yellow teardrop or 1 large yellow tomato**
- ☐ **1 red onion**
- ☐ **fresh rosemary**
- ☐ **fresh chives**
- ☐ **fresh thyme**
- ☐ **selection seasonal fresh fruit**

PANTRY CHECK

Check the pantry before you leave home to make sure that you have the following ingredients on hand, if not add them to your shopping list.

- ☐ **honey**
- ☐ **mayonnaise**
- ☐ **wholegrain mustard**
- ☐ **balsamic or red wine vinegar**
- ☐ **white wine**
- ☐ **garlic**

MENU PLANNER

- ☐ **Turn oven on.**
- ☐ **Prepare marinade.**
- ☐ **Place lamb in marinade and set aside to marinate for 10 minutes.**
- ☐ **Cook lamb.**
- ☐ **Make dressing for Asparagus tied with Leeks. Cover and refrigerate.**
- ☐ **Make Tomato and Thyme Salad. Cover and refrigerate.**
- ☐ **Prepare Asparagus tied with Leeks and set aside.**
- ☐ **Prepare Smoked Salmon and Brie.**
- ☐ **Cook Asparagus tied with Leeks.**
- ☐ **Remove ice cream from freezer and place in refrigerator to soften.**

Previous page: Tomato and Thyme Salad, Honey Rosemary Lamb, Asparagus tied with Leeks
Plates Waterford Wedgwood
Opposite: Smoked Salmon and Brie

SMOKED SALMON AND BRIE

125 g/4 oz smoked salmon slices
125 g/4 oz Brie cheese, sliced
4 slices rye bread, toasted and cut
in half
1/2 avocado, stoned, peeled and sliced
1 tablespoon lime juice
freshly ground black pepper

Arrange salmon and Brie cheese on toast. Top with avocado and sprinkle with lime juice and black pepper to taste.

Serves 4

Keep a selection of paper napkins on hand that match your china and you will always be able to colour coordinate your table.

Plates Waterford Wedgwood

HONEY ROSEMARY LAMB

Oven temperature
200°C, 400°F, Gas 6

Lamb racks are available from supermarkets and good butchers. If they are already prepackaged and contain more than 3 cutlets each, simply cut to the correct size.

4 racks of lamb, each containing 3 cutlets, trimmed of all visible fat

ROSEMARY HONEY MARINADE
**2 tablespoons chopped fresh rosemary
or 1 teaspoon dried rosemary
3 tablespoons honey
2 cloves garlic, sliced
$^1/_2$ cup/125 mL/4 fl oz white wine**

1 To make marinade, place rosemary, honey, garlic and wine in a large bowl and mix to combine. Add lamb, turn to coat and set aside to marinate for 10 minutes.

2 Remove lamb from marinade, place in a greased baking dish and bake for 20 minutes or until lamb is cooked to your liking.

Serves 4

ASPARAGUS TIED WITH LEEKS

**500 g/1 lb asparagus spears, trimmed
1 thin leek, quartered lengthwise**

MUSTARD DRESSING
**$^1/_2$ cup/125 g/4 oz mayonnaise
2 tablespoons wholegrain mustard
2 tablespoons snipped fresh chives
freshly ground black pepper**

1 To make dressing, place mayonnaise, mustard, chives and black pepper to taste in a bowl and mix to combine. Cover and refrigerate until ready to serve.

2 Divide asparagus into four portions and tie each with a strip of leek. Steam or microwave asparagus until tender. Drain and serve topped with a spoonful of dressing.

Serves 4

If asparagus is unavailable green beans can be prepared in this way.

Good quality purchased ice cream followed by truffles and coffee is the perfect end to a meal.

TOMATO AND THYME SALAD

125 g/4 oz cherry tomatoes, halved
2 plum (egg or Italian) tomatoes,
quartered
125 g/4 oz yellow teardrop tomatoes,
halved or 1 large yellow tomato,
chopped
$^1/_2$ red onion, sliced
2 tablespoons chopped fresh thyme
3 tablespoons balsamic or red
wine vinegar
$^1/_2$ teaspoon sugar
salt

Place cherry tomatoes, plum (egg or Italian) tomatoes, yellow tomatoes, onion, thyme, vinegar, sugar and salt to taste in a salad bowl and toss to combine. Cover and refrigerate until ready to serve.

Serves 4

Purchase truffles or florentines from the bakery section of your supermarket or a local bakery. Check out the confectionary and biscuit sections of the supermarket; there are some excellent packaged items that are delicious to have with coffee and are good to have on hand for impromptu entertaining.

Plates, cups and saucers Waterford Wedgwood

WINTER CELEBRATION

MENU
Salmon Frittata

Creamy Chicken Stir-fry
Peppered Pasta

Citrus Sponge Pudding

One of the secrets to successful impromptu entertaining is presentation. Remember, use your good china and cutlery, take a little extra time to arrange food attractively and use simple garnishes.

SHOPPING LIST
Take this list with you when you go shopping and you won't have to worry about forgetting an important ingredient.
- ☐ 220 g/7 oz canned pink or red salmon
- ☐ 4 boneless chicken breast fillets
- ☐ 315 g/10 oz sour cream

FRUIT AND VEGETABLES
- ☐ 4 spring onions
- ☐ assorted lettuce leaves
- ☐ 250 g/8 oz button mushrooms
- ☐ 250 g/8 oz snow peas (mangetout)
- ☐ 1 red pepper
- ☐ 2 lemons
- ☐ 1 orange

PANTRY CHECK
Check the pantry before you leave home to make sure that you have the following ingredients on hand, if not add them to your shopping list.
- ☐ 6 eggs
- ☐ 500 g/1 lb fettuccine
- ☐ wholegrain mustard
- ☐ butter
- ☐ milk
- ☐ crushed black peppercorns
- ☐ vegetable oil
- ☐ dry white wine
- ☐ chicken stock
- ☐ Parmesan cheese
- ☐ caster sugar
- ☐ self-raising flour
- ☐ desiccated coconut

MENU PLANNER
- ☐ **Turn on oven.**
- ☐ **Prepare and cook pudding.**
- ☐ **Preheat grill.**
- ☐ **Prepare and cook frittata.**
- ☐ **Prepare and cook Creamy Chicken Stir-fry.**
- ☐ **Cook pasta.**

Peppered Pasta,
Creamy Chicken Stir-fry

CREAMY CHICKEN STIR-FRY

2 teaspoons vegetable oil
4 boneless chicken breast fillets, sliced
250 g/8 oz button mushrooms, sliced
$^{1}/_{2}$ cup/125 mL/4 fl oz dry white wine
$^{1}/_{2}$ cup/125 mL/4 fl oz chicken stock
315 g/10 oz sour cream
250 g/8 oz snow peas (mangetout),
trimmed
1 red pepper, sliced

1 Heat oil in a wok or frying pan over a high heat, add chicken and stir-fry for 3 minutes. Add mushrooms and cook for 2 minutes longer or until chicken is tender. Remove chicken mixture from pan and set aside.

2 Stir wine and stock into pan and bring to simmering over a medium heat. Simmer for 5-10 minutes or until liquid reduces by half. Reduce heat to low, slowly whisk in sour cream and cook for 1 minute.

3 Add snow peas (mangetout) and red pepper to pan and cook for 2 minutes. Return chicken mixture to pan and simmer for 2 minutes longer or until heated through.

Serves 4

PEPPERED PASTA

500 g/1 lb fettuccine
3 teaspoons crushed black
peppercorns
15 g/$^{1}/_{2}$ oz butter
2 tablespoons grated Parmesan cheese

Cook pasta in boiling water in a large saucepan following packet directions. Drain well, add black peppercorns, butter and Parmesan cheese to hot pasta and toss to combine.

Serves 4

The addition of a bowl of flowers, fresh fruit or candles gives your dinner table a festive appearance.

Salmon Frittata

SALMON FRITTATA

4 eggs, lightly beaten
$^1/_2$ cup/125 mL/4 fl oz milk
2 teaspoons wholegrain mustard
freshly ground black pepper
2 teaspoons vegetable oil
4 spring onions, chopped
220 g/7 oz canned pink or red
salmon, drained
2 teaspoons grated lemon rind
assorted lettuce leaves

1   Place eggs, milk, mustard and black pepper to taste in a bowl and whisk to combine. Set aside.

2   Heat oil in a nonstick frying pan over a medium heat. Add spring onions and cook, stirring, for 1 minute. Add salmon and lemon rind and spread out evenly over base of pan.

3   Pour egg mixture into pan and cook over a low heat for 5 minutes or until frittata is almost set.

4   Place pan under a preheated hot grill and cook for 3-4 minutes or until top is golden. To serve, cut into wedges and accompany with assorted lettuce leaves.

Serves 4

For a very simple table decoration place a small flower or herb sprig on each table napkin.

Plates Waterford Wedgwood

Plate Waterford Wedgwood

CITRUS SPONGE PUDDING

Oven temperature
180°C, 350°F, Gas 4

1 cup/220 g/7 oz caster sugar
$^1/_2$ cup/60 g/2 oz self-raising flour
3 tablespoons desiccated coconut
1 tablespoon finely grated lemon rind
1 tablespoon finely grated orange rind
2 tablespoons lemon juice
2 tablespoons orange juice
2 eggs, separated
125 g/4 oz butter, melted and cooled
1 cup/250 mL/8 fl oz milk

1   Place sugar, flour, coconut, lemon rind and orange rind in a bowl and mix to combine.

2   Beat in lemon juice, orange juice, egg yolks, butter and milk. Place egg whites in a bowl and beat until stiff peaks form.

3   Fold egg whites into citrus mixture and pour into a greased 1 litre/$1^3/_4$ pt capacity ovenproof dish. Place in a baking dish, with enough hot water to come half way up the sides of the dish and bake for 45 minutes or until cooked.

Serves 4

This dessert is delicious served with cream or ice cream.

INDEX

ACKNOWLEDGMENTS

The publisher thanks the following companies who generously supplied props for this book.

Corso de Fiori
335 South Dowling St,
Darlinghurst, Sydney
Ph: (02) 360 5151
Also Crown St, Surry
Hills and Sky
Gardens, City

Country Road
Homewear Stores
nationally and
selected Myer/Grace
Bros stores

Orrefors Kosta Boda
available from
Orrefors Kosta Boda
Corporate Stores,
David Jones and
selected stores

Pillivuyt
Available from
selected stores and
distributed by Hale
Imports
97-99 Old Pittwater
Rd, Brookvale,
Sydney
Ph: (02) 938 2400
enquiries only

G & C Ventura
60 Justin St, Lilyfield,
Sydney
Ph: (02) 555 7277
enquiries

Waterford
Wedgewood
Australia Limited
Available from major
department stores
and leading specialty
stores
Ph: (02) 899 2877
enquiries only